C201 134062

D0246763

A Day in the Life: Polar Animals

Narwhal

LIBRARIES NI
WITHDRAWN FROM STOCK

Katie Marsico

www.raintreepublishers.co.uk
Visit our website to find out more information about Raintree books.

To order:
☎ Phone 0845 6044371
🖨 Fax +44 (0) 1865 312263
✉ Email myorders@raintreepublishers.co.uk

Customers from outside the UK please telephone +44 1865 312262

Raintree is an imprint of Capstone Global Library Limited, a company incorporated in England and Wales having its registered office at 7 Pilgrim Street, London, EC4V 6LB – Registered company number: 6695582

Text © Capstone Global Library Limited 2012
First published in hardback in 2012
The moral rights of the proprietor have been asserted.

All rights reserved. No part of this publication may be reproduced in any form or by any means (including photocopying or storing it in any medium by electronic means and whether or not transiently or incidentally to some other use of this publication) without the written permission of the copyright owner, except in accordance with the provisions of the Copyright, Designs and Patents Act 1988 or under the terms of a licence issued by the Copyright Licensing Agency, Saffron House, 6–10 Kirby Street, London EC1N 8TS (www.cla.co.uk). Applications for the copyright owner's written permission should be addressed to the publisher.

Edited by Daniel Nunn, Rebecca Rissman, and Sian Smith
Designed by Joanna Hinton-Malivoire
Picture research by Hannah Taylor
Original illustrations © Capstone Global Library
Production by Victoria Fitzgerald
Originated by Capstone Global Library Ltd
Printed and bound in China by South China Printing Company Ltd

ISBN 978 1 406 22885 4 (hardback)
15 14 13 12 11
10 9 8 7 6 5 4 3 2 1

Belfast & South Eastern Library Service

British Library Cataloguing in Publication Data

Marsico, Katie, 1980-
Narwhal. – (A day in the life. Polar animals)
1. Narwhal – Juvenile literature.
I. Title II. Series

Belfast & South Eastern Library Service	
C201 134062	
Askews & Holts	08-Mar-2012
599.543	£10.99

Acknowledgements
We would like to thank the following for permission to reproduce photographs: Corbis p. 6 (Paul Nicklen); FLPA pp. 4 (Minden Pictures/ Flip Nicklin), 7, 23c (Minden Pictures/ Flip Nicklin), 11 (Minden Pictures/ Flip Nicklin), 12 (Minden Pictures/ Flip Nicklin), 17 (Sunset), 19 (Minden Pictures/ Flip Nicklin), 22 (Minden Pictures/ Flip Nicklin); Getty Images pp. 5, 23g (Paul Nicklen), 8, 23b (Paul Nicklen), 9 (Rudi Sebastian), 16 (Minden Pictures/ Flip Nicklin), 18 (Minden Pictures/Flip Nicklin), 20, 23d (Minden Pictures/ Flip Nicklin), 21 (Minden Pictures/Flip Nicklin); Photolibrary pp. 13, 23f (Waterframe Images), 14 (Robert Harding), 15 (Oxford Scientific/Doug Allan); SeaPics.com pp. 10, 23a (© John K.B. Ford/Ursus).

Front cover photograph of a narwhal and back cover photograph of a narwhal's tusk reproduced with permission of Getty Images (Paul Nicklen). Back cover photograph of a tail reproduced with permission of Corbis (Paul Nicklen).

The publisher would like to thank Michael Bright for his assistance in the preparation of this book.

Every effort has been made to contact copyright holders of material reproduced in this book. Any omissions will be rectified in subsequent printings if notice is given to the publisher.

Disclaimer
All the Internet addresses (URLs) given in this book were valid at the time of going to press. However, due to the dynamic nature of the Internet, some addresses may have changed or ceased to exist since publication. While the author and publishers regret any inconvenience this may cause readers, no responsibility for any such changes can be accepted by either the author or the publishers.

Contents

What is a narwhal?. 4

What do narwhals look like? 6

Where do narwhals live?. 8

What do narwhals do in the day? 10

What do narwhals eat?. 12

What hunts narwhals?. 14

Do narwhals live in groups?. 16

What do narwhals do at night? 18

What are baby narwhals like? 20

Narwhal body map. 22

Glossary. 23

Find out more 24

Index 24

Some words are shown in bold, **like this**.
You can find them in the glossary on page 23.

What is a narwhal?

A narwhal is a **mammal** that lives in icy **polar** waters.

All mammals have some hair on their bodies and feed their babies milk.

tusk

Narwhals are whales.

Males have a long tooth called a **tusk** on their upper jaw.

What do narwhals look like?

tail

Narwhals have flippers and a tail.

Most have spotted skin.

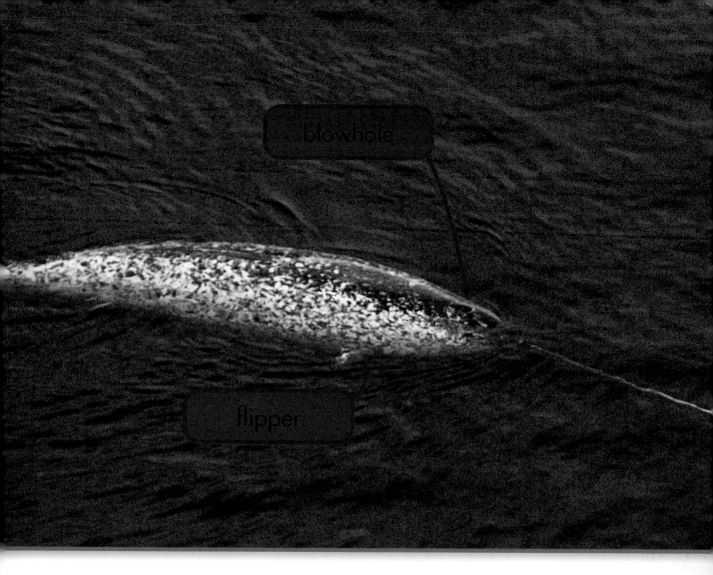

blowhole

flipper

Narwhals also have a **blowhole** at the top of their head.

They use the blowhole to breathe in air at the surface of the water.

Where do narwhals live?

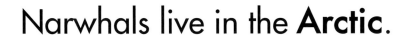

Arctic

Narwhals live in the **Arctic**.

In the Arctic it is light all day and all night for part of the summer.

In the Arctic it is dark all day and all night for part of the winter.

The Arctic is one of the coldest places in the world!

What do narwhals do in the day?

Narwhals are **active** during the day and at night.

They spend part of the day searching for food deep in the ocean.

Narwhals spend some time resting near the surface of the water.

They need to breathe in air before they dive down to search for food.

fish

Narwhals eat fish, shrimp, and squid.

They often catch their food deep in the ocean, where it is very dark.

Narwhals make sounds that bounce back and tell them where things are.

This is called **sonar**.

What hunts narwhals?

killer whale

Killer whales hunt and eat narwhals.

Polar bears and walruses also attack them.

People hunt narwhals, too.

They kill the whales for their **tusks** and skin.

Do narwhals live in groups?

Narwhals live in groups called pods.

This helps them to keep safe from their enemies.

There are usually about 15 to 20 narwhals in a pod.

Narwhals travel together and communicate by using sounds such as clicks and whistles.

What do narwhals do at night?

Narwhals spend a lot of the night diving for food.

They can dive down into very deep parts of the ocean.

Narwhals sometimes rest in between dives at night, just as they do in the day.

People are still trying to find out more about how narwhals sleep.

What are baby narwhals like?

calf

A mother narwhal gives birth to a baby about once every three years.

Baby narwhals are called calves. They are a blue-grey colour.

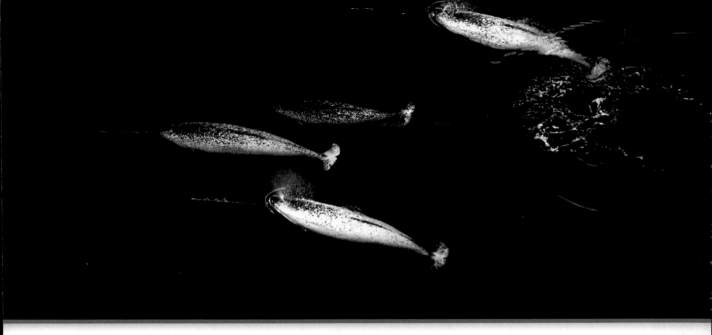

A calf lives with its mother for one or two years while it drinks her milk.

Then young narwhals are ready to join a pod and go hunting in icy waters!

Narwhal body map

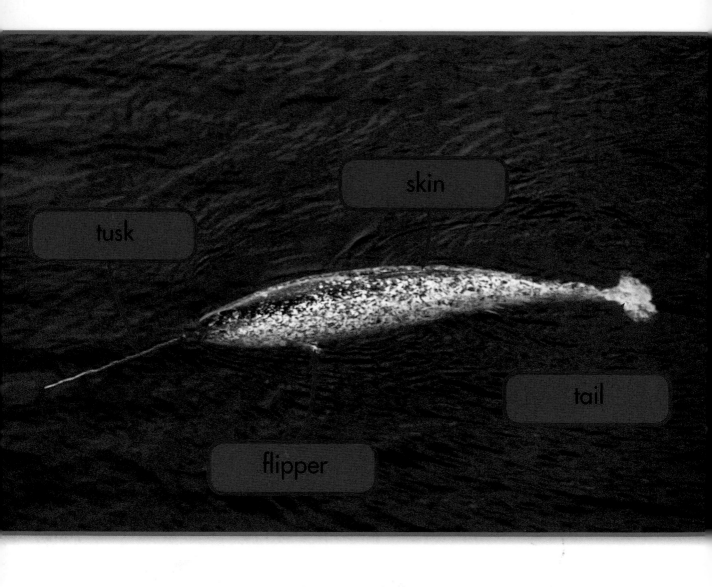

skin

tusk

tail

flipper

Glossary

 **active** busy doing lots of things

 **Arctic** area surrounding the North Pole. It is very cold in the Arctic.

 **blowhole** hole at the top of a narwhal's head used for breathing air

 **mammal** animal that feeds its babies milk. All mammals have some hair or fur on their bodies.

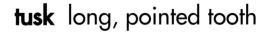 **polar** extremely cold areas at the top and bottom of the world

 **sonar** a system that uses sound to find objects

 **tusk** long, pointed tooth

Find out more

Books

Arctic and Antarctic (Eye Wonder), Lorie Mack (DK Publishing, 2006)
Whales of the Arctic, Sara Swan Miller (PowerKids Press, 2009).

Websites

**video.kids.nationalgeographic.com/video/player/
kids/animals-pets-kids/wild-detectives-kids/wd-ep4-
narwhaltooth.html**
Watch a video of narwhals on the National Geographic website.

**www.sciencenewsforkids.org/articles/20060125/
Feature1.asp**
Find out about a narwhal's tooth at Science News for Kids.

Index

Arctic 8, 9
enemies 14, 15, 16
feeding 10, 11, 12, 18
groups 16, 17
mammal 4
polar 4

rest 11, 19
skin 6, 15, 22
sonar 13
sounds 13, 17
tusk 5, 15, 22
young 4, 20, 21